'A Dangerous Book.
Encourages Obesity and
excess sex . . .
. . . Highly Recommended.'
*Jasper Carrott.*

# The Dieter's Guide to Weight Loss During Sex

Richard Smith

*Text illustrations by David English*

Arrow Books

## Acknowledgement

THERE ARE MANY TO WHOM I AM
INDEBTED, BUT THEY WISH, ALAS, TO
REMAIN ANONYMOUS.

Arrow Books Ltd
3 Fitzroy Square, London W1P 6JD

An imprint of the Hutchinson Publishing Group

London Melbourne Sydney Auckland
Wellington Johannesburg and agencies
throughout the world

First published in Great Britain
by Souvenir Press Ltd 1978
Arrow edition 1980

Set in Monotype Times New Roman

Made and printed in Great Britain by
Hazell Watson & Viney Ltd,
Aylesbury, Bucks

ISBN 0 09 921890 9

# Contents

## 4 Intercourse and Things Related

## 5 Afterwards

## 6 Supplementary Activities

## 7 Miscellaneous Problems, Emergencies and Disasters

## 8 Eating and Sex (The Bedside Eater)

## 9 The Height Report

# Introduction

*'If you like exercise, you will like this book. If you loathe exercise, you will love this book.'* ANONYMOUS

How much weight do we lose during sex? Although the diet literature abounds with charts and books explaining how many calories we burn while jogging, playing tennis or golfing, similar information concerning sexual activity has, until now, been largely unavailable. Yet, a random survey of 206 million Americans indicates that 98 percent devote more time and effort to sex than to jogging, tennis or golf, and we felt the time right for a book explaining why.

In the past, efforts to determine weight loss during sex usually met with failure, possibly due to the ignorance of researchers and their poor choice of subjects. One experiment, for example, to determine calories burned during foreplay, ended abruptly when both participants fell asleep, their mutual lack of interest attributable to a fifty-six year age difference. Another misguided experiment, an attempt to prove that regular sexual activity (a minimum of 74.2 times a week) could tighten the waistline and perk up one's tennis game collapsed when, on the fourth day of the experiment, the battered participants went insane. As a result, the lack of reliable data made it impossible for the average person to calculate weight loss while removing clothing, fumbling around or attempting a truly satisfying orgasm in an un-heated tent.

With few exceptions, sex is considered to be the least boring and most pleasurable form of physical exercise, not to mention the cheapest. Indeed, those who indulge have nothing but praise for its all-around benefits and vigorous endorsements such as, 'I like it' ... 'It's nice' ... 'It beats walking to Uruguay in moccasins', are not uncommon. Standard exercises, of course, are effective weight-shedders but they take a good deal of time. One hour of jogging, for example, burns only 600 calories; one hour of swimming, 500 calories (more if you remain underwater); and two hours of pitch 'n' putt only 71. On the other hand, faking an orgasm convincingly can burn as many as 160 calories in just nineteen seconds, not counting the warm-up. Add to this another twenty calories for avoiding the wet spot and thirty calories for getting a towel and the benefits of sexual activity become obvious—everything we do burns calories and two hours of enthusiastic sex can easily burn off a pastrami sandwich, a slice of pecan pie, two scoops of ice cream and those few maverick cellulites on your upper thigh. Thus, by thinking of sexual activity in terms of calories burned, we can calculate how much weight we lose, using 3500 calories to the pound. The more activity, of course, the more weight lost.

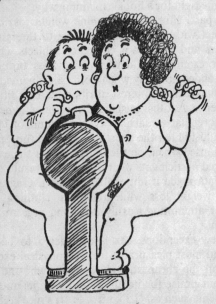

In this handbook, we have attempted to cover every conceivable aspect of sex, thereby showing you at a glance the dramatic impact chronic sexual activity has not only on the body, but on the mind as well. Although the most modern scientific methods have been used to ensure accuracy, the problems confronted were, to say the least, profound. The calories burned, for example, while trying to find a more comfortable position, will vary greatly according to whether you are comfortably ensconced on a king-size bed or scrunched in the back of a Japanese sedan. Furthermore, despite the wonders of the electronic age, the task of translating emotional reactions such as rage, disappointment, herpes and anxiety into calories-burned was such that careful estimates had to do. And finally, during the heat of passion, despite the fact that the electrodes would constantly fall off, the frenzied participants simply refused to stop and our figures had to be adjusted accordingly.

We therefore suggest that you use this book as an informal guide rather than a rigid manual, making necessary caloric adjustments according to your own individual size and temperament, plus the length of time you indulge, how you indulge and whether or not you have a partner. Once you have reached your ideal height and weight, you may still continue sexual activity without worrying about adverse side effects such as brooding or excessive slimness.

The ability of sexual activity to induce weight loss is perhaps best illustrated by the fact that one hour of heavy petting, including squirming, wiggling and whimpering for more, can easily burn off the caloric equivalent of either five shots of Creme de Menthe or a double portion of birthday cake. See the following chart for additional examples.

| Sexual Activity | Burns off |
| --- | --- |
| 1 hour of intensive foreplay (114 breaths per minute) or 18 minutes of intercourse | 1 slice (large) of chocolate cake |
| 26 minutes of nonstop intercourse plus one 9-minute orgasm, or the equivalent | 2 slices of pizza with extra cheese, meatballs and mushrooms |

| | |
|---|---|
| 16 minutes of frisking and tickling partner | 9 lollipops |
| 53 minutes of French kissing or 25 minutes of normal foreplay or 6 minutes of abnormal foreplay | 1 cheeseburger with 14 french fries and a dollop of ketchup |
| 2 hours of bondage or 47 minutes of flogging using a medium-weight flog | 2 bottles of beer, large portion of spaghetti and 1 slice of toast |
| 7 minutes of aural sex (anything involving partner's ear) | 1 Cadbury's Flake (no wrapper) |
| 15 minutes of oral sex | 11 grapes |
| 52 minutes of massaging partner's back or 10 minutes of massaging your own back | 1 wedge of crab quiche Lorraine with 1 glass of wine |

| | |
|---|---|
| 1 hour of stomach to stomach resuscitation | 1 piece of fudge (generous) |
| 62 minutes of chasing partner around the room at a medium jog, or a 2-hour pillow fight with 20-pound pillows | 1 pint of ice cream |
| 1 sneeze | 12 bean sprouts (salted) |
| 14 minutes of fondling | Chocolate mousse: stingy portion |
| Intercourse in at least 4 different positions within 6 minutes | Chocolate mousse: huge portion |
| 31 minutes of foreplay in the lotus position | 2 Cornish pasties with wild rice and pudding |
| 24 minutes of mutually satisfying oral sex in a swimming pool | 1 large slice of cheesecake |

# 1

---

# Preparing for
# Your Partner

The road to perfect sex begins with a perfect you. In addition to showing how much weight you lose while preparing for your partner, this section is designed to help you make sure that you are physically and mentally ready for even the most gruelling sexual activity. For your guidance, we have listed below some questions frequently asked by people about to have sex. Use the information in the following pages to resolve any problems.

- Am I strong enough?
- Do I doubt my ability to satisfy?
- Does my heart pound just from fluffing up the pillows?
- Am I satisfied with my biceps? triceps? quadriceps? eyesight?
- Can I carry my partner into the bedroom without making a fool of myself?
- How's my complexion?
- All pimples well hidden?
- Are my toenails a sight? Are my toes aligned?
- Is anxiety causing lower abdominal distress?
- Should I eat now, or later?
- Should I take a Valium?
- Do I really need this?
- Will it be fun?
- Will it be meaningful?
- If it's meaningful, will it still be fun?

# Physical Conditioning

*'A sound mind in a fat body slips around.'*
  M. TITO FARTSEK, Ph D

It is during sex that our bodies do, or at least try to do, the most magical and wonderful things. We grab and grope, slide and squirm, reach and stretch, strain our muscles and perform feats of agility that would flabbergast an ape. Yet, instead of adequately preparing ourselves for such fervent activity, most of us think nothing of just jumping into bed without so much as a push-up, touching the toes or hopping up and down.

Along with ligament problems, this lack of preparation can lead to premature exhaustion, the first signs of which are shortness of breath, a feeling of dizziness if you lie down too fast, failure to respond to partner's strokes and an intense desire to do nothing but stare at television. And all this after just four minutes of foreplay. The result will be a sense of inadequacy and profound lethargy, a condition that may persist for as little as two hours or as long as several days, during which time it may be difficult to walk, pour juice and chew inexpensive cuts of meat. In addition, the habitually sedentary, especially those with a chronic aversion to exercise, will, in all likelihood, experience a massive cramp.

It is obvious that being out of shape can ruin, even wreck, and possibly destroy one's sex life. According to the President's Council on Physical Fitness, a need to nap after heavy exertion such as running up an inclined surface, orgasm or making stew suggests that one's condition is less than tip-top and an exercise programme might be in order.

The following modest exercises, while by no means representing a total conditioning programme, will prove helpful in overcoming sexual inertia, improving virtuosity and building the stamina to cope with any partner, no matter where or how well they were trained.

# Basic Exercises

*(Each exercise to be performed at least one hour before sex)*

| *Activity* | *Calories burned* |
| --- | --- |

**Push-ups (five)** ...................................... 14
General strength, firms upper arms and shoulders,
increases ability to hold on when on top of partner,
also makes it easier to remove a partner who has
fainted on top of you.

**Sit-ups (five)** ....................................... 10
Tones and strengthens vital stomach muscles,
enabling you to quickly leap out of bed should
something go wrong. Also makes sitting up in bed
easier should you wish to eat, watch television or
glance at the time.

**Reverse sit-ups (three)** ........................... 563
For super strength. Do exactly what you would do
for a regular sit-up except lie face down on the floor.

**Touch toes (ten)** ..................................... 7
Smashes fat deposits, increases flexibility. Permits
you to dabble with positions that would normally
damage your spine. Also lets you reach for things such
as food and sedatives without straining.

**Touch waist (ten)** ................................... $\frac{1}{2}$
For those not yet loose enough to reach all the way
to their toes. Similar effect as above but less—far less.

**Arm curls (five, using comfortable weight)** .............. 9
Builds strong biceps, inspires confidence and
occasionally makes vaccination mark more
prominent. A must for those who wish to lift their
partner at the crucial moment and gallantly carry
them into the bedroom. Without this exercise,

17

instead of confidently lifting your partner, it is likely that you will fall to the floor and begin groaning piteously. This exercise is especially useful to the understrength woman with spindly arms who'd like to beat her partner at arm wrestling.

---

Squeezing a rubber ball (twenty squeezes) ..............3

During sex, a strong grip is needed for everything from extending a hearty handshake to picking up fruit. It is especially vital for clinging to your partner should things get really good. For the woman who wants to win skirmishes or have her partner in her power during tickling sessions, a secure grip is essential.

---

Jogging (at least one mile) .........................100

The ultimate all-around exercise for increasing stamina and firming many of the muscles used during sex. Also enlarges lung capacity and increases oxygen efficiency, allowing you to hold your breath (should you have to) for prolonged periods of time.

*The following exercises are optional.*

Handstand . . . . . . . . . . . . . . . . . . . . . . . . . . . . . . . . . . . . . . . . . . . .40
Difficult, but most rewarding. Keeping knees
straight, bend over from the waist and place palms
flat on the floor. Take two small steps forward. You
should now be standing on your hands. Hold for the
count of ten.

Floor touch . . . . . . . . . . . . . . . . . . . . . . . . . . . . . . . . . . . . . . . . . . .50
Stand with arms at sides. Without bending knees
or moving feet, slowly and gracefully lean forward and
touch forehead to the floor. Remain there, count
to two, and return to original position. Those with
yoga training will have little trouble.

Side bend . . . . . . . . . . . . . . . . . . . . . . . . . . . . . . . . . . . . . . . . . . . .20
Clasp hands behind neck and drop to knees.
Slowly bend sideways and touch right shoulder to
floor. Remain ten seconds, then return to original
position. Repeat for left shoulder.

There are, of course, additional methods of achieving erotic fitness. These include such vigorous exercise as tennis,
skiing, bicycling, backgammon and sleeping on a camp bed.
All are excellent for increasing cardiorespiratory endurance
and perking up one's sexual performance.

# Mental Conditioning

It is impossible to enjoy sex if depressed, not in the mood or the mind is distracted by everyday cares. For now, you must strive for a feeling of well-being; worries about stock losses, overdue dental bills and a grievously ill plant must be put aside. The following are common methods of cleansing the mind, dissipating tension and achieving serenity.

| Activity | Calories burned |
|---|---|
| Transcendental meditation | 4 |
| Incidental meditation | 1 |
| (*takes less time—can be done while brushing teeth*) | |
| Self hypnosis | 9 |
| Psychoanalysis (per session) | 17 |
| If analyst makes house calls | 12 |
| Prayer | 5 |
| Watching an X-rated movie | 7 |

If it's a grainy print and you have to squint, add three calories. If the sound track is blurred and you have to put forth extra effort to hear, that's another two calories.

| | |
|---|---|
| Calling a parent | 3 |
| Frisking a ham (to help get you in the mood) | 3 |
| Biofeedback | 6 |

If you don't have the proper equipment, just plug your fingers into your ears and listen to your hands. It really works!

# Personal Grooming

| Activity | Calories burned |
| --- | --- |
| Showering | 8 |
| Taking a bath | 6 |

Drying hair
    With towel (vigorously) .......................... 9
    Blow drying. ....................................... 3
    Using cheeks .................................... 348
       *(deduct 4.96 calories if bald)*

Brushing teeth. ....................................... 2
With electric toothbrush ........................... $\frac{1}{4}$

Inspecting face for pimples, blemishes, etc .............. 2
    *(Includes paranoiac reaction to grape-size zit about to
    debut on bridge of the nose.)*

Shaving (either sex). ................................. 3

Applying cosmetics (either sex). ...................... 3

Selecting clothing
    If you care ........................................ 7
    If you don't ....................................... 1

# 2

# Setting the Scene and Initial Intimacy

Creating an atmosphere of intimacy and comfort will immediately put your partner at ease and in the mood for sex. Ambience, therefore, is everything. If you have a fireplace, light it. If it's August, don't. Check the bed. Is it strong enough? In good repair? Any joints need regluing? Is the kitty litter changed? Has the dog been gently chloroformed? Children all gone to Aunt Mabel's? Any threatening photos in view? Parrot gagged? Record albums ready? Refrigerator stocked? Plenty of ice? Bathroom looking its best? Sure, it's a lot of trouble. But the result will be a satisfied partner who will willingly and without complaint take the garbage on the way out.

# Preparing the Bedroom

| Activity | Calories burned |
|---|---|
| If you're fussy | 42 |

*(Give or take three calories).*

Includes dusting, fluffing up the pillows, tuning the radio, bouncing up and down on the bed, putting up posters and setting the snooze alarm. Make sure the lighting is right—too dark and the place becomes a coal mine; too light and it looks like an operating room. Try a 25-watt candle. Avoid assertive incense. Use props such as books to make a good impression and show what kind of a person you are. Books of poetry, for instance, convey literacy and sensitivity. They should be conspicuously placed—on the dresser, by the night table and perhaps one or two under the covers. Besides poetry, select a few books that give the impression that you are unusual— slightly eccentric but not quite certifiable—thus adding to the mystery of the sexual experience. A few suggested titles: *Remedial Norwegian, The Romance of Welding* (Vol. II), *Build Your Own Mailbox, Jingles of the Japanese* (for those who like Haiku) and *Happy Porkchops, The Story of a Cheerful Butcher.*

**Note:** If someone extra special is coming, you may want to change the sheets, or at least flip them over. Add another four calories for either activity.

# Preparing the Bathroom

Even under normal everyday circumstances, the bathroom should be regarded as a holy place, a sanctuary for cleansing the body, renewing the spirit and occasionally hiding from the world. During sex, however, the bathroom also becomes a first aid station. It should therefore be spotless, sparkling and filled with such amenities as soft, fluffy towels, a cheerful shower curtain, a new bar of soap with a muted aroma, an extra toothbrush and a toilet that flushes with a soothing pleasant whoosh. If possible, we suggest boiling the entire bathroom, just to be certain. If this is not convenient, see the following:

| *Activity* | *Calories burned* |
|---|---|
| Erasing two-month-old ring from bathtub | 11 |
| Scrubbing (de-crudding) tiles | 14 |
| Removing alien vegetation from shower curtain | 12 |
| Replacing towels | 3 |
| Installing new roll of toilet paper | 2 |

Security is a fresh roll of toilet paper in the dispenser plus five backup rolls.

| | |
|---|---|
| Scraping excessive soap buildup from soap dish | 4 |
| Disinfecting bath mat | 6 |
| Tidying medicine chest | 3 |

Will prevent hundreds of jars, bottles and brushes from crashing into the sink when partner gets aspirin.

| | |
|---|---|
| Hiding other toothbrush | 1 |

# Additional Last-Minute Preparations

| Activity | Calories burned |
| --- | --- |
| Vacuuming | 6 |
| Hiding sex manual | 3 |

*(If you're still not sure of what to do, write the answers on your cuffs.)*

| | |
| --- | --- |
| Decanting wine | 4 |
| If you don't have a corkscrew | 268 |

*(Not only does this process allow the wine to breathe, but it prevents your partner from discovering that your modest—but acutely drinkable—Bordeaux only cost £1.00, including the bottle.)*

| | |
| --- | --- |
| Putting on CHICKEN INSPECTOR button | 1 |

# Getting Partner in Mood and Alerting Mutual Sensibilities

*(Wait until your partner arrives before commencing any of the following.)*

| Activity | Calories burned |
|---|---|
| **Reciting poetry** | |
| Shelley (Percy Bysshe) | 3 |
| Lord Byron | $3\frac{1}{2}$ |
| Rossetti | 4 |
| Milton | 8 |
| Berryman | 12 |
| McKuen | $\frac{1}{2}$ |

| Reading *War and Peace* aloud (no rest stops) | 1573 |
|---|---|

| **Practical jokes** (a good change of pace) | |
|---|---|
| Whoopie cushion | 11 |
| Squirting flower | 14 |
| Fake teeth | 7 |
| Joy buzzer | 10 |
| Exploding cigar | 20 |

All of the above are not only in impeccable taste, but great for breaking the ice.

| **Ribald jokes** | |
|---|---|
| Dirty | 8 |
| Filthy | 14 |

| **Listening to music** | |
|---|---|
| Light classical | 3 |
| Heavy classical | 5 |
| Chamber music | 10 |
| Opera: Mozart | 15 |
| Verdi | 27 |
| Wagner | 248 |
| Muzak | 20 |

*To all categories above add five calories if tapping feet.*

Dancing

Dancing close together is a good way to get a sneak preview of your partner's body tone and decide if you wish to go any further.

Showing a silent horror film while dressed in rubber knickers and a strange hat . . . . . . . . . . . . . . . . . . . . . . . . . . . . . . .18
  (*slightly kinky, check with your partner before renting a projector*)

Reading the Bible together . . . . . . . . . . . . . . . . . . . . . . . . .10

Playing doctor . . . . . . . . . . . . . . . . . . . . . . . . . . . . . . . . . . . . .8

# Communicating

| *Activity* | *Calories burned* |
|---|---|
| Meaningful conversation | see below |

Naturally, the shorter and less imaginative the conversation, the less energy used and the fewer calories burned. Beginning a conversation with, 'I've got nothing to talk about, let's go to bed,' though certainly direct, burns only three calories and may alienate the most willing partner. The longer and deeper the conversation, however, the harder your imagination works and the more calories consumed. A discussion of camel pasturalism in New Jersey or Einstein's paper on emotional distress in birds can burn as many as fifty calories and make you feel important. See the following topic suggestions for substantial caloric consumption.

| | |
|---|---|
| Wishing rickets on your boss | 24 |
| How you are striving to become your own person | 28 |
| How you are striving to become the person your parents meant you to be | 35 |
| How you are trying to become less dependent on your: mother/father/niece/butcher | 57 |
| All of the above | 268 |
| The echoes of Nietzsche in 'Jingle Bells' (*light philosophy is always surefire*) | 75 |
| Spelling Nietzsche correctly without looking it up | 92 |
| Should science attempt to put a man on the sun? | 60 |
| Is it moral to drive while fully asleep? | 33 |
| Zen Buddhism and Lo Mein: | |
| Which is more fulfilling? | 37 |
| Which is more filling? | 40 |

# Making the First Move

| Activity | Calories burned |
|---|---|
| If you are shy | 15 |
| If you have a morbid fear of success | 22 |
| If you are easily intimidated when a person acts distant and reserved | 36 |
| A person who orders you to keep your hands to yourself is acting distant and reserved. | |
| If you are an anxious person with a large inferiority complex | 45 |
| If you sell used cars | 2 |
| If you politely ask your partner if it's okay to put your arm around him/her | 17 |
| (*so ridiculous that it sometimes works*) | |
| If you beg | 25 |

According to psychologists, the anxiety produced by the prospect of making the first move, for either sex, is directly proportional to one's fear of asking a delicatessen waiter for a clean glass.

# Overcoming Resistance

| Activity | Calories burned |
|---|---|

**Passive** . . . . . . . . . . . . . . . . . . . . . . . . . . . . . . . . . . . . . . . . . . . . . . $1\frac{1}{2}$

Passive resistance indicated if partner, while
trembling, utters 'don't' in a low, meek voice.
'Please don't stop' indicates extremely passive
resistance.

---

**Active** . . . . . . . . . . . . . . . . . . . . . . . . . . . . . . . . . . . . . . . . . . . 62

Active resistance may include biting, punching and
weapons. Press on if you think it's only an act.

---

Seducing partner (only applies to venal partners)
   If you are rich . . . . . . . . . . . . . . . . . . . . . . . . . . . . . . . . . . . . . . . 5
   If you are poor . . . . . . . . . . . . . . . . . . . . . . . . . . . . . . . . . . . . . . 164

# Body Contact and Initial Touching

| Activity | Calories burned |
| --- | --- |
| Fumbling | 4 |
| Casually rummaging around | 7 |
| Gentle rubbing | 10 |
| Serious fondling | 14 |
| Involved massaging | 17 |
| Caressing | 19 |

Petting
    Above the waist under loose-fitting garment
    such as sweater or raincoat ... 21
    Below the waist under tight ski pants ... 46
    (*stop if the waistband cuts off your circulation*)

Squeezing (any part of body except entire head) ... 15

# Kissing

| Activity | Calories burned |
|---|---|
| Gentle | 10 |
| Heavy | 17 |
| Passionate | 26 |
| *(Giving partner's shirt collar a love bite, for example.)* | |
| Actually sucking blood | 41 |
| Recovering shape of nose | 11 |
| French kissing | |
|    With mouth open | 18 |
|    With mouth closed | 239 |
|    Tongue strain | 65 |
| Dutch kissing (applies only if you're Dutch) | 24 |
| Kissing various areas of body | |
|    Uvula | 11 |
|    Soft palate | 9 |
|    Eyelid | 3 |
|    Retina | 8 |
|    Liver | 37 |
|    Lungs | 30 |
|    Back of nose | 66 |
|    Wrist | 12 |
|    Watch | 10 |

# Removing Clothes

| Activity | Calories burned |
| --- | --- |
| With partner's consent | 12 |
| Without partner's consent | 187 |
| In winter | 25 |

Calorie count provides for removal of typical cold-weather gear—ski parka, shirt, pants, hat, earmuffs, scarf, gloves, long underwear, goggles, socks and boots.

| | |
| --- | --- |
| In summer | 3 |

*Miscellaneous*

Removing socks by violently shaking feet ............418
*(Very impractical and seldom works, but for those interested in high weight loss, it's essential.)*

Unhooking bra
Using two calm hands ...........................7
Using one trembling hand .......................96
*(The record here for incompetence is two and a half hours and a badly mutilated index finger.)*

Any attempt to remove tights without
first removing slacks.............................375
*(Add another one hundred calories if you are actually successful.)*

Should you remove all of your clothes? The answer is generally yes, since most people take it as a sign of commitment. Women are especially put off by men who keep their socks on and also by men who, being unduly obsessed with hygiene, refuse to have sex unless permitted to keep their pants on. There are also those who find it difficult to even temporarily part with a lucky charm, and it is not unusual for people to have sex while clutching a rabbit's foot or portable radio. It is, however, generally acceptable to wear adornments to bed such as earrings, rings, crosses, Jewish stars, ankhs and perfume.

# Arousal and Stimulation (advanced)

It was difficult to assign caloric values in this category, since what is high-kilowatt sex for some may be total boredom for others. One person, for instance, may respond sexually to a pork chop; another, instead, may eat it. And there are those who do not consider the phrase 'urban renewal' erotic. We therefore freely admit that the counts below are somewhat imprecise.

| Activity | Calories burned |
| --- | --- |
| Blowing in partner's ear | |
|    Using mouth | 9 |
|    Using bellows | 14 |
|    Using blow dryer (low setting) | 2 |
| Blowing in your own ear | 158 |
|    (*Experimental form of autoeroticism still not completely tested*) | |
| Nibbling on partner's earlobe | 8 |
|    (*If your partner is a gypsy, be careful not to swallow an earring*) | |
| Biting partner's head | 27 |
| Lust | 15 |
| Talking dirty | 8 |

# Weight Loss Bonus No. 1

| Activity | Calories burned |
| --- | --- |
| Striptease | 55 |

If you are even marginally graceful, stripping to music presents an excellent opportunity to lose weight while arousing your appreciative and leering partner. It also gives you a chance to take your clothes off yourself, instead of worrying about the quivering hands of someone who is desperately trying to remove your new fifty pound French dungarees, despite the fact that you still have your boots on. You must be careful, however, not to ruin the erotic mood by attempting something unsuitable and that might cause you to look foolish. Overweight women would do well to avoid body movements that require excessive swinging and swaying, or leaping. *A grand jeté* or a hula is not a good choice.

| | |
| --- | --- |
| Belly dancing | 100 |
| Actually dancing with partner's belly | 165 |

**Note:** Unless you are obsessively neat, wait until afterwards to hang up your clothes and insert shoe trees.

# Weight Loss Bonus No. 2

| Activity | Calories burned |
|---|---|
| Stage fright ........................................ | 18 |

Can occur when both partners are finally naked and realize they will soon have to quit stalling and get on with it. Chief symptoms of stage fright are anxiety, nausea and an irrational need to either sleep or flee. It can usually be conquered by locking yourself in the bathroom and releasing the 'bad energies' with a plunger.

# Embarrassment

Calorie counts indicate amount of energy expended when coping with feelings of embarrassment and disgrace induced by:

| Activity | Calories burned |
| --- | --- |
| Large juice stain on shorts | 10 |
| Holes in underwear | |
|   If you are rich | 2 |
|   If you are poor | 20 |
| Excessive hair in unusual places | |
|   Pubic hair extends to feet | 25 |
|   Hair around nipples (for man) | $\frac{1}{2}$ |
|   (for woman) | 8 |
| Cellulites | 12 |
| Large pores | 10 |
| Tattoo with raised lettering | 18 |
| Bloodshot nose | 14 |
| Bags over the eyes | 66 |

# Disappointment

Clothing can conceal and lie, causing many people to feel disappointed, even cheated, upon seeing their partner naked. In some cases, a less intimate activity may be preferred, such as watching a game show. A man who looks great in a suit turns out to have shoulders only eight inches wide, a chest like a raisin and legs like bleached sticks. A woman removes her shoes, shrinks from 5'7" to 4'9" and no one can find her. The following are some common disappointments and the calories burned in dealing with them:

| *Activity* | *Calories burned* |
| --- | --- |
| Partner looked better with clothes on | 10 |
| (*You may prefer sex with your partner's clothes.*) | |
| Partner looks better with your glasses off. | 10 |
| Partner's body resembles a tubercular chicken | 12 |
| Partner wears corrective underwear | 15 |
| Partner's sweater turns out to be hair on his/her chest | 20 |
| Partner turns out to be of wrong sex | 100 |
| You don't mind | $\frac{1}{2}$ |
| Partner turns out to be of wrong religion | 57 |
| Partner wears elevated shoes | 12 |
| Partner wears elevated socks | 50 |
| Typical reactions to sexual disappointment | |
| Setting bed on fire | 8 |
| Setting partner on fire | 15 |
| Suicide | 1 |
| Profound depression | 9 |

Inventing complicated but believable excuse for
leaving ('I have to go,' is one example) ................5

# Getting into Bed

| Activity | Calories burned |
| --- | --- |
| Lifting partner | 15 |
| Straining | 20 |
| Turning red | 5 |
| Deciding who sleeps on the good side of the bed (the side closest to the kitchen) | 14 |

No longer male-dominated activities. Many a woman, especially the strong, silent type, will take pride in lifting her partner, carrying him into the bedroom and gently tossing him onto the bed. Men appreciate this gesture, especially if they're tired and have to go to work, although there may be a few who feel threatened.

| | |
| --- | --- |
| For those not strong enough for the above procedure, drag your partner along the floor | 16 |
| Using skateboard | 3 |
| Shivering from cold sheets | 9 |
| Shivering from fear | 19 |
| Setting snooze alarm | 1 |
| Placing teeth in glass of water (*applies only if they're false or very loose*) | 3 |
| Saying prayers | 1 |
| Tucking each other in | 547 |

One couple got in and out of bed 137 times before realizing that it couldn't be done.

# 3

---

# Foreplay

'You've got to start somewhere.'
    DR SHIRLEY EINSTEIN,
    NOTED THERAPIST

Professional dieters tell us that one burns more calories
during foreplay than during any other stage of sex, with the
possible exception of dancing in a tweed grope suit or intercourse in the back-to-back position. It is easy to see why.
Foreplay is a time to experiment and try new things—magic
caresses with a kipper, love bites if you have good teeth,
bouncing with abandon and ricocheting off the wall and
arousing each other by making ridiculous faces.

Those, on the other hand, who regard foreplay as drudg-
ery may prefer to skip directly to intercourse and hope their
partner won't notice.

# Ten Alternate Erogenous Zones

*(Should regular zones temporarily wear out)*

1. Back of lips
2. Between the toes
3. Either bicuspid
4. Either vocal cord
5. Calluses
6. The taste buds
7. Any unpolished nail
8. The pinky ring
9. Any part of the endocrine system
10. Third shelf of the refrigerator

# Being Good in Bed

Information here is for preparation only. Detailed descriptions and specific calorie counts are covered in the rest of the chapter.

*The ideal male partner*

- Willingly pitches in
- Lasts a long time before orgasm
- Is not distracted by fog, hiccups or reprimands
- Does quite well in at least six different positions
- Gives partner multiple orgasms
- Gives himself multiple orgasms
- Has a sense of timing which permits simultaneous orgasm
- Doesn't keep asking, 'How am I doing?'
- Doesn't scold partner or grow sullen is she gets dressed and leaves
- Cheerfully gives post- and pre-coital back rubs
- Screams and yells only in bed
- Always removes his watch

# Being Good in Bed

*The ideal female partner*

- Doesn't mind if partner gives her multiple orgasms
- Lasts only two minutes before first orgasm
- Doesn't wake the neighbours
- Enjoys being aggressive
- Doesn't feel used if partner collapses after four hours of sex
- Doesn't make a face during oral sex
- Lets partner do anything within reason
- Doesn't keep asking, 'How are you doing?'
- Stays awake throughout
- Is attentive to partner after orgasm
- Can administer first aid
- Has plenty of food in the refrigerator
- Doesn't say 'poor baby' if man has an orgasm while switching off the light

# Being Even Better in Bed

| Activity | Calories burned |
|---|---|
| Honestly telling partner what gets you excited | 5 |

# Going Too Far

| Activity | Calories burned |
|----------|----------------|
| Calming horrified partner ........................... | 163 |

# Writing

*(An excellent muscle-loosener)*

| Activity | Calories burned |
| --- | --- |
| From | |
|   Pleasure | 12 |
|   Pain | 12¼ |
|   Tickling | 16 |
|   *(Add five calories if partner is holding you down.)* | |
|   Cramps | 9 |
|   Something you ate | 20 |

*Additional muscle looseners*

| | |
| --- | --- |
| Somersaults | 15 |
| Gross contortions | 28 |

# Teasing

When done in moderation, teasing your partner with a tongue (preferably yours) can be highly erotic and an effective calorie burner.

| Activity | Calories burned |
|---|---|
| Licking partner all over but being careful to avoid all sexually sensitive areas ............................20 *(With hairy partners, it will be necessary to periodically pause and dredge the mouth.)* | |
| Constantly resisting frustrated partner who is desperately trying to push your head towards sexually sensitive areas ............................35 | |

**Note:** Overdoing this procedure will cause your partner to become peevish and attempt to direct your tongue to sensitive areas by grasping and pulling on it, and not caring whether your head goes along.

# Stroking

| Activity | Calories burned |
|---|---|
| With | |
|   Feather | 4 |
|   Hand | 6 |
|   Tips of fingers | 7 |
|   Tips of toes | 68 |
|   Sausage | 15 |
|   Suede cat-o'-nine-tails | 22 |
|   Fly swatter | 14 |
|   Nervous dog | 50 |
|   Magic Marker | 11 |

# Oral Sex

| Activity | Calories burned |
| --- | --- |
| Cunnilingus | 15 |
| Nosebleed<br>(*can be caused by over-excited partner*) | 5 |
| Fellatio<br>(*Requires almost twice the effort of cunnilingus since it uses more muscles, especially those of the neck, hands and eyes.*) | 30 |
| Attempting to breathe through a severely stuffed nose | 14 |
| Hat trick | 187 |
| Toe sucking | 12 |
| With shoes on | 49 |

One of the great advantages of oral sex is that if both partners are in fairly good health, it can go on almost indefinitely. The only adverse side effects will be a temporary lapse in the efficiency of the taste buds and difficulty in chewing anything harder than apple sauce.

# Removing Hair

| Activity | Calories burned |
|---|---|
| From tongue | 3 |

A relatively simple operation involving thumb and index finger. Try to be discreet.

| From roof of mouth | 8 |
|---|---|

Slightly more complicated. Finger and tip of tongue may be necessary.

| From soft palate | 14 |
|---|---|

Very complicated, especially if it is sticking. You may have to use tongue plus a couple of fingers, possibly even your whole fist. If this doesn't work, try a fork.

| From uvula | 20 |
|---|---|

If hair is wrapped around uvula, it is easily extractable with pliers or a vacuum cleaner. Partner may notice.

| From throat | 23 |
|---|---|

Unless there's a small mop handy, you're better off just swallowing the hair. Only two calories per strand, no matter what the colour.

# Disposing of Hair

Once you have successfully extracted the hair, you must dispose of it without offending your partner. ('Love me, love my hair.') Jettisoning it over the side of the bed would seem logical, except that a strand of hair is so light that it will probably stick to your fingers. You'll end up shaking your hand violently and accomplishing nothing except destroying the mood. Consider the following options:

| *Activity* | *Calories burned* |
| --- | --- |
| Surreptitiously wiping it on sheet . . . . . . . . . . . . . . . . . . . . . . .1 | |
| Wiping it on partner . . . . . . . . . . . . . . . . . . . . . . . . . . . . . . .3 *(A good idea, but the hair may come back to haunt you.)* | |
| Putting it back where you found it . . . . . . . . . . . . . . . . . . .28 *(The drilling motions may disturb your partner.)* | |

**Note:** We suggest hiding it underneath your arm until later.

# Achieving Erection

| Activity | Calories burned |
| --- | --- |
| For normal healthy man | $2\frac{1}{4}$ |
| For normal healthy woman | 549 |
| For man who is forty-six, folds his clothes neatly and still lives with his mother | 78 |
| *(especially if she's waiting downstairs in a taxi)* | |

# Sustaining Erection

| Activity | Calories burned |
| --- | --- |
| For man | 4 |
| For woman | 163 |

Some men consider this to be a woman's responsibility and just lie there, hoping that something will happen. For the woman this is good, since fighting gravity gives her the chance to burn lots of calories. One woman reports that she spent three hours trying to arouse a timid deacon, during which time she lost two pounds but grew so weak that her life began to flash before her eyes.

# Weight Loss Bonus No. 3

| Activity | Calories burned |
| --- | --- |
| Losing erection | $\frac{1}{4}$ |
| Searching for it | 115 |

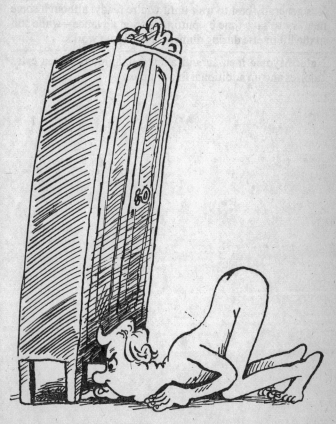

# Putting on Prophylactic

| Activity | Calories burned |
| --- | --- |
| With erection | $1\frac{1}{4}$ |
| Without erection | 300 |

It is generally best to wait until you're ready, although some men try to save time by putting it on in advance—while still in the lift or else during dinner. This seldom works.

**Note:** Myopic men should allow a minimum of ten extra calories and an additional five minutes.

# Inserting Diaphragm

| Activity | Calories burned |
| --- | --- |

If woman who does it is
   Experienced ........................................6
   Inexperienced ....................................73
   If man does it regardless of experience .............680
Add five calories for retrieving it from across the room—
add 100 if you leave it there.

# Delays

| Activity | Calories burned |
| --- | --- |
| Frigidity | 11 |

*Some common causes:*

- Partner is wearing 'Days of the Week' boxer shorts and garters
- Partner's foreplay technique consists of lighting a cigar and ordering food from Kentucky Fried Chicken
- Partner refuses to show you his vasectomy scar
- Fear of feeling obligated
- Hunger pangs and you've just eaten
- Partner keeps asking, 'Are you there yet?'
- Television too loud
- Television too soft
- Lack of privacy (maid keeps running in and asking for milk and biscuits)
- Brim of partner's hat keeps hitting your forehead
- Large oil painting of Karl Marx on ceiling

# Further Delays

| *Activity* | *Calories burned* |
| --- | --- |
| Impotence | 11 |

*Some common causes:*
- Desire to be trendy
- Subtle defence mechanism against giving or receiving VD.
- Senility
- Harassment by a large dog
- Three-minute time limit
- Eight glasses of wine
- Fear of success
- Sixth attempt in an hour
- Hangover
- Partner's locket, when she's on top, keeps going in your mouth

**Note:** So long as neither partner gets upset, there is nothing to worry about and sex should proceed as if everything were normal.

# Emotional Distress

| Activity | Calories burned |
| --- | --- |

Emotional distress ...............................22

A mild breakdown—hysteria, withdrawal, sitz baths, etc.—is a common and often pleasant reaction to an attack of impotence or frigidity.* If you are basically healthy, however, there is little to worry about unless your partner exhibits hostile behaviour by picking up the phone and inviting someone better to come over. You will then spend the next two months wandering around in slippers and pajamas and eating frozen meals without defrosting them.

---

*Those who suffer from impotence *and* frigidity should see a doctor of some sort.

# 4

# Intercourse and Things Related

Intercourse usually follows directly after foreplay, except in the case of extremely spirited foreplay, in which case it might be wise to wait a day or two. Since intercourse puts such a severe strain on our physical and mental resources, we should be alert to the twelve warning signs of sexual enfeeblement:

1. Indifference to Renaissance architecture
2. Manic lips
3. A ringing in the mouth
4. Fingers won't snap
5. Palpitating liver
6. Loss of all sensation below hairline
7. A morbid craving for steak
8. Vastly improved high notes
9. Change of blood type
10. Herniated salivary gland
11. Persistent need for juice
12. Motion sickness

# Doing It for the First Time

Don't panic if the earth doesn't move. The first time around is usually more intellectual than physical. Many people, in fact, find themselves drawn to the word 'fiasco' when called upon to describe their initial experience. 'Catastrophe,' 'botch,' 'tragedy' and 'lawsuit' are also sometimes used. Most problems, however, dissolve with time, patience and two or three hundred partners' worth of experience. Indeed, it is not unusual for the sexually gifted to go from hideous incompetence to blatant greatness within a four-year period. Following are some first-time problems:

| *Activity* | *Calories burned* |
| --- | --- |
| Fumbling around | 4 |
| Desperately trying to put something somewhere | 18 |
| Completely missing | 9 |
| Embarrassment | 15 |
| Disappointment (the famous 'You mean that's it?' syndrome) | 27 |
| Scorn | 30 |
| Any traumatic episode<br>Inadvertently, but expertly bringing pillow to orgasm | 60 |
| Partner dozes off | 41 |

# Doing It for the Last Time

Following are the calories burned according to the most common reasons for swearing off intercourse.

| Activity | Calories burned |
| --- | --- |
| New Year's resolution | 15 |
| Age | |
|     Too old | $1\frac{1}{2}$ |
|     Too young | $1\frac{1}{4}$ |
| Something better happens along | 5 |
| Lack of time | 11 |
| Religious conversion | 15 |
| Discovering that intercourse detracts from foreplay | 22 |
| Bed repossessed | 16 |

# Doing It

| Activity | Calories burned |
|---|---|
| Deciding position | |
| Tossing coin | 2 |
| Cutting cards | 2½ |
| Eenie meenie meiny murray | 3 |
| Attempting insertion | |
| Using hands | 4 |
| Using feet | 500 |
| While still deciding position | 288 |

# Insertion

# Insertion

| Activity | Calories burned |
| --- | --- |
| If woman is ready | $\frac{1}{4}$ |
| If man is not | 274 |

# Satisfying Partner

*(Organ size)*

Most experts agree that size means nothing. Shape is what counts, and the man with an H-shaped organ can write his own ticket. In those rare instances where a man has a genuinely small member,* he may have to compensate by working slightly harder, but this is good for weight loss. A man with a really large organ,† while he might not have to work as hard once inside, may exhaust himself just trying to convince his partner to let him put it inside.

| Activity | Calories burned |
|---|---|
| Normal size | 22 |
| Oversize | 15 |
| Tremendous | 8 |
| Teensy-weensy | 163 |

*¼ to ½ inch
†2 feet and up

# Positions

Constantly experimenting with new positions not only presents an opportunity to show off, but also lets you exercise the body, lose weight and rescue your sex life from monotony. Happily, the number of possible positions is nearly infinite, even more if you use a foot stool. The Royal Academy of Tibet recognizes over 860,* the Turkish Book of Delights lists 525 and the United Nations officially sanctions 203. It would be a rare couple indeed who couldn't find at least ten fully functional and highly satisfying ways to show each other that they care. Mentioned below are but a few of the more popular positions, all of which combine maximum weight loss with productive body contact. Select those that work best for you and don't be discouraged if it takes a little time to get them perfect.

| *Activity* | *Calories burned* |
|---|---|
| Man on top, woman on bottom (facing each other) ......20 | |
| Man on top, woman on bottom (back to back) ........749 | |
| Woman on top, man on bottom ......................25 Many women find that in addition to its inherent sexual possibilities, this position affords a better view of the clock. | |
| Standing Both partners of equal height ......................18 Woman one foot taller than man ...................90 (*The man will have to make several rigorous leaps into the air in order to achieve even minimal satisfaction.*) | |

*804 are quite useless, however, unless you already are a helpless cripple and have nothing left to lose.

    A slight variation on the so-called reverse
    missionary position; the adventuresome will find it
    amusing. While on top, the woman raises her left
    thigh and places it behind her neck, all the while
    rotating her pelvis until she is spinning out of
    control, thus inducing her partner to feel useful.
    Not only is this position visually agreeable, but it
    permits the woman to reach an impressive climax
    without actually snapping her spine. (Not
    recommended for those convalescing.)

    Accomplished with the man on his knees, thighs
    spread, his elbows resting on a pillow, his head
    against the wall. The woman then approaches from
    the rear and wonders what to do.

# Positions According to Nationality

74

# Locations

*(Additional calorie counts for places other than bed.)*

| Activity | Calories burned |
|---|---|
| In suburbia | 3½ |
| On a bar stool | 20 |
| Rear of a Mini | 38 |
| In a call box<br>Standing | 14 |
| Lying down | 274 |
| On a lawn chair (plastic webbing) | 88 |
| Under a pyramid | ? |
| On an airliner<br>Aisle seat | 24 |
| Middle seat (fat passenger on either side) | 42 |
| Window seat | 30 |
| In the lavatory | 100 |
| In a hammock (on a breezy day) | 50 |

Add 25 calories if only one end is tied to tree.

| In a van with bad springs | 11 |
|---|---|

It should also be noted that pleasure is heightened when sex takes place spontaneously—during a movie, during Lent, while backing out of the driveway, etc.

# Intercourse

| Activity | Calories burned |
| --- | --- |
| Starting (overcoming inertia) | 4 |
| Moderate (sort of gliding along) | 15 |
| Heavy (enthusiastically involved) | 27 |
| Merciless pounding | 50 |
| Incoherent convulsions | 75 |
| Shock | 100 |
| Blacking out | 125 |
| Hernia | 150 |
| Heart attack | 227 |
| Death | 1 |

# Possible Side Effects of Intercourse

| Activity | Calories burned |
| --- | --- |
| Bouncing | 7 |
| Sliding around | 9 |
| Serious skidding | 12 |
| Full cartwheel | 20 |
| Whiplash | 27 |
| Knee burn | 6 |
| Chafed elbows | 5 |
| Chafed nose | 11 |

# Sex-Related Noises

| Activity | Calories burned |
| --- | ---: |
| Giggling | 7 |
| Laughing | 11 |
| Short gasps (per gasp) | 3 |
| Wheezing | 5 |
| Squeals | 4 |
| Ecstatic moaning | 11 |
| Low growling | 8 |
| Squishing | 10 |
| Shouting | 16 |
| Screaming | 18 |
| Urgent begging | 22 |
| Any short speech giving partner directions | 25 |

('*Please don't stop*,' '*Just a little more*,' '*Faster*,' '*One
inch more and make a sharp right*' are common
examples)

If it embarrasses you that your neighbours might hear,
merely stuff partner's mouth with any citrus fruit.

# Seeking Comfort

| Activity | Calories burned |
| --- | --- |
| Switching positions | 16 |
| Without stopping | 41 |

Unless you have nonskid sheets, the slipping and sliding caused by sexual activity may result in a good deal of lateral movement, and you may end up in some extraordinarily uncomfortable and totally unworkable positions.*

Changing positions is advised should any of the following occur:

- You find yourself teetering at the edge of the bed and a vicious dog with paws akimbo is waiting for you to fall.
- One of you actually falls off the bed. (If you continue to have intercourse, add one hundred calories.)
- You suddenly discover that one of your shoulders is on the bed and the other is touching the floor.
- You've moved up too far and your head is repeatedly slamming into the wall in time to the thrusts, making it difficult to concentrate and keep your tiara on.
- One leg has become so entangled in the sheets that the foot is turning green and gangrene appears imminent.
- A stupendous thrust blasts you both through the window, thereby putting all chances of a really satisfying orgasm in jeopardy.

---

*In extreme cases, couples can cover as many as four miles during three hours of really intensive sex. One couple, after starting out in the bedroom, found themselves, two hours later, dodging bowling balls in the third lane of Archie's Bowl-O-Rama on League Night. They were upset.

# Approaching Orgasm

| Activity | Calories burned |
|---|---|
| Letting go | $5\frac{1}{2}$ |
| Controlling yourself | 79 |
| Digging nails into back | |
|     Your partner's | 11 |
|     Your own | 165 |
| Shifting gum | 1 |
| Chewing faster | 2 |
| Much faster | $3\frac{1}{2}$ |
| Trembling | 15 |
| Shaking | 20 |
| Shuddering | 25 |
| Trying to keep eyes open | 33 |

# Orgasm

| Activity | Calories burned |
| --- | --- |
| Real | 27 |
| Faked | 160 |

# Orgasmic Intensity Scale

| Activity | Calories burned |
| --- | --- |
| Shoes flew off | 35 |
| Expression didn't change | ½ |
| Room turned purple | 4 |
| Face turned purple | 15 |
| Orchestra swelled | 6 |
| Birds sang | |
|     Large birds | 7 |
|     Small birds | 3 |
| Magical explosions | 10 |
| Trumpets blared | 12 |
| Flutes blared | 2 |
| Roman candles | 14 |
| Blazing pinwheels | 16 |
| Blazing sheets | 25 |
| Earth moved | 30 |
| Vesuvius erupted | 47 |
| You began moaning in Latin | 60 |

# Pulling Out

(*Un-insertion*)

| Activity | Calories burned |
| --- | --- |
| After orgasm | $\frac{1}{4}$ |
| A few moments before orgasm | 500 |

# Multiple Orgasms for Female

| Activity | Calories burned |
| --- | --- |
| Two | 14 |
| Five | 30 |
| Eight | 47 |
| Fifteen | 106 |

Depending on greed—and her rate of recovery—a woman can enjoy up to eight orgasms within a one-hour period without losing consciousness or disarranging her hair. As the number increases, however, she may begin to experience a form of 'reduced sanity' that will temporarily interfere with her ability to cook, worship and ride a Moped.

# Multiple Orgasms for Male

| Activity | Calories burned |
| --- | ---: |
| Two | 21 |
| Three | 39 |
| Four | 57 |
| Twelve | ?* |

For a man, it's a different situation, perhaps due to physiological and biological reasons. Many men can enjoy up to four orgasms in an hour with little discomfort except for a slight ringing in the ears. With few exceptions, however, a man who tries to achieve more than ten orgasms within that same period is flirting with irreversible brain damage.

*Subject lapsed into a coma too soon afterward to tell.

# Special Orgasms

| Activity | Calories burned |
| --- | --- |
| Clitoral | 15 |
| Vaginal | 21 |
| Penile | 21 |
| Scrotile | 15 |
| Rectal | 25 |
| Oral *(can also occur during an especially good meal)* | 30 |
| Futile | 1 |

# Premature Ejaculation*

(*For male*)

| Activity | Calories burned |
| --- | --- |
| During insertion . . . . . . . . . . . . . . . . . . . . . . . . . . . . . . . . . . . . . . . . .2 | |
| During intercourse . . . . . . . . . . . . . . . . . . . . . . . . . . . . . . . . . . . . . . .5 <br> (*approximately two seconds or three thrusts after insertion, whichever comes first*) | |
| During foreplay . . . . . . . . . . . . . . . . . . . . . . . . . . . . . . . . . . . . . . . . .3 <br> (*while scrambling eggs, for example*) | |
| During dinner (very premature) . . . . . . . . . . . . . . . . . . . . . . . .1 | |
| While parking the car (over-anticipation) . . . . . . . . . . . . .¼ | |
| Immature ejaculation . . . . . . . . . . . . . . . . . . . . . . . . . . . . . . . . . .4 <br> (*similar to premature ejaculation except male acts childish and throws a tantrum*) | |

*Often caused by an inability to do things right.

# Consequences of Premature Ejaculation for Female

Even if you have a good heart, it takes much understanding not to feel like a victim when your partner climaxes after three seconds of intensive sex, especially if he immediately sits up to watch the Cup final.

| Activity | Calories burned |
| --- | --- |
| Frustration | 8 |
| Anger | 15 |
| Violent mood swing | 20 |
| Suppressing rage | 25 |
| Not suppressing rage | 65 |

In extreme cases, this can include cursing, nose tweaks, and gently massaging partner's head with a tyre iron.

**Note how unfair:** Men never seem to mind if a woman has an orgasm after three seconds of sex.

# Consequences of Premature Ejaculation for Male

| Activity | Calories burned |
| --- | --- |
| Cursing | 10 |
| Apologizing | 3 |
| Snivelling | 5 |
| Pleading for mercy | 8 |
| Begging for another chance | 15 |

# Achieving Orgasm Under Unusual Circumstances

| Activity | Calories burned |
| --- | --- |
| While donating blood | 45 |
| After two bottles of wine | 50 |
| *(Even insertion may be a problem.)* | |
| While talking on the telephone | 15 |
| On a mushy bed | 11 |
| With close relatives in the room | 60 |
| While negotiating for a loan | 100 |
| During a job interview | 100 |
| During intercourse | 8 |

# Delaying Orgasm

Medical evidence suggests that prolonged procrastination of orgasm (four to six weeks) impedes the flow of vital juices, making you feel bloated and not at peace with the world. Delaying orgasm for a reasonable time, however, causes little harm and may be necessary in order to accommodate a slow partner. A man whose partner has been repeating the phrase, 'not yet,' over a two-hour period will find it necessary to hold off. At a certain point, though, he will become desperate and wonder if he's going to die. Women, occasionally, find it convenient to postpone orgasm if they think they're going to hate themselves in the morning or, at the very latest, right after lunch. Following are some tips on how to delay orgasm without leaving the room:

- Think about your teeth.
- Rethink the Middle East crisis.
- Take a pencil and total a recent supermarket receipt either on the pillowcase or your partner's forehead.

# 5

# Afterwards

What happens directly after sex can be just as important as what happened during. Some people immediately light a cigarette. Others immediately put theirs out. Generally, however, most people concentrate on making their partner feel that it was totally satisfying and wonderful. This is easily accomplished by just lying there and looking contented (a vapid stare is good), instead of rushing into the bathroom and scrubbing yourself with Ajax.

# Weight Loss Bonus No. 4

| Activity | Calories burned |
|---|---|
| Avoiding the wet spot | 20 |

# Things Often Said After Sex

| Activity | Calories burned |
| --- | --- |
| All post-coital utterances .............................15 | |

Examples:
  'Continue sedation!'
  'Your wig is on backwards.'
  'Was it good for you?'
  'I'm so grateful.'
  'It must have been something we ate.'
  'Don't do that again.'
  'How's it going?' (also said during intercourse)
  'I've got such a headache.'
  'Get out.'
  'Congratulations.'
  'Are you finished?'
  'Am I finished?'
  'It's a miracle.'
  'You did it wrong.'
  'I'm exhausted.'
  'Please help me.'
  'When do we eat?'

# Possible Side Effects of Good Sex

The first indication that sex was a positive experience will be a buzzing in the pelvic area and a clear complexion. You might also feel pleasantly light, as though you were dozing in a vat of cream cheese. If sex was really terrific, you feel dangerously drained, as though your body had been connected to a large milking machine for several days. Additional reactions include:

| Activity | Calories burned |
|---|---|
| Swooning | 6 |
| Palpitations | 10 |
| Shortness of breath | 5 |
| Perspiring | 8 |
| Amnesia | 22 |
| Bronchitis | 25 |
| Mild gum damage | 12 |

# Possible Side Effect of Bad Sex

| Activity | Calories burned |
| --- | --- |
| A less-than-sunny disposition ..........................1 |

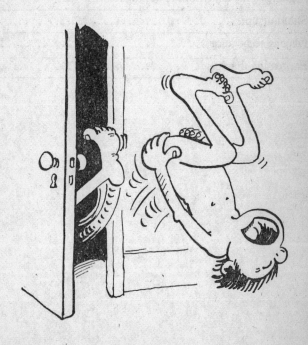

# Recovering

| *Activity* | *Calories burned* |
|---|---|
| Un-entwining | 3 |
| Regaining motor control of pelvis | 7 |

After especially tiring sex, you may feel numb from below the waist to the opposite wall. The result will be an inability to walk (put one foot in front of the other), which will seriously impair your chances of going to the bathroom or getting food.

| | |
|---|---|
| Standing up | 9 |
| Getting some juice | 11 |
| Expressing thanks | 2 |

# Rolling Over and Going to Sleep

| Activity | Calories burned |
| --- | --- |
| After intercourse | 18 |

Classic behaviour for shiftless men who believe they've done their job and are now entitled to a rest. This 'rest' may include snoring.

| Activity | Calories burned |
| --- | --- |
| During intercourse | 32 |

Women find this to be a subtle, yet direct way of suggesting dissatisfaction.

| Activity | Calories burned |
| --- | --- |
| During foreplay | 12 |

Indicates either an advanced case of fatigue or a serious lack of interest.

| Activity | Calories burned |
| --- | --- |
| While still in the kitchen | 5 |

Situation hopeless.

| Activity | Calories burned |
| --- | --- |
| Rolling over and falling off the bed | 2 |

# Sleep

| Activity | Calories burned |
| --- | --- |
| Real | 5 |
| Faked | 74 |

A good way to avoid a sex-crazed partner who simply won't give up. Faking sleep is also a reliable escape technique when, after sex, you suddenly find yourself wishing that you could make your partner disappear. This may happen when you go to bed with somebody just for sex, which is a sin.

# Trying Again

# Tidying and Cleaning Up

| Activity | Calories burned |
|---|---|
| Racing partner to bathroom | |
| Barefoot | 6 |
| In floppy slippers | 18 |
| In sloppy flippers | 50 |

# Showering

| Activity | Calories burned |
| --- | --- |
| Alone | 7 |

*(To burn extra calories, hold the soap perfectly still and move your body.)*

| Activity | Calories burned |
| --- | --- |
| With partner | 12 |
| With a waterpik | 133 |
| With no hot water | 187 |

*(includes writhing and making hideous faces)*

| Activity | Calories burned |
| --- | --- |
| Taking a bath together | |
|   In the bath | 5 |
|   In the basin | 28 |
| Damp mopping each other | 10 |
| Brushing each other's teeth | 25 |

# Drying Off

# Making the Bed

| Activity | Calories burned |
|---|---|
| With partner still in it | 44 |

(*Indicates either a neatness obsession, a severe optic disorder or a partner who is very tired.*)

| | |
|---|---|
| With you still in it | 97 |

(*Suggests extreme withdrawal and profound dissatisfaction.*)

| | |
|---|---|
| Mending furniture | 22 |
| Rinsing sheets | 25 |
| Just shaking them out | 15 |
| Removing candle wax | 10 |

# 6

---

# Supplementary Activities

So much activity is compressed into sex that we sometimes fail to realize that weight loss is going on constantly, and sometimes when we least expect it. Did you know, for instance, that fantasizing can burn an additional twenty calories, even more if you despair? Or that a depraved bondage-and-scolding session may actually reduce your waistline? In this section we will see how the so-called fringe areas of sex can play an important role not only in caloric consumption, but in making sex something special.

# Male Fantasies

Fantasy can be used for anything from enhancing an already terrific sexual experience to blocking out a dull partner and concentrating on something more pleasant. Surviving eight minutes with a trucker named Earl who talked you into bed over his CB radio, for example, might be accomplished by fantasizing about sex with a polished Nazi who sings Wagner in your ear. Following are some common sexual fantasies and the calories burned while thinking about them.

| *Activity* | *Calories burned* |
| --- | --- |
| Sex slave to five insomniac starlets | 18 |
| Sex with a Quaker named Natasha | 14 |
| Casual intercourse with a warm bugle | 9 |
| Foreplay with a skittish frog | 11 |
| 'Love wrestling' with an elk | 22 |
| Sex with a chicken wearing a tiny rubber raincoat | 15 |
| Making love to bread | 5 |
| Sex in a knapsack (constrictus claustrophobus) | 12 |

# Female Fantasies

| Activity | Calories burned |
| --- | --- |
| Wild intercourse with a jolly butcher | 20 |
| Foreplay with a hallucinating accountant | 17 |
| Doing it in downtown Sheboygan | 40 |
| Getting ravished by a senator | 9 |
| An afternoon in bed with a caring dolphin | 15 |
| Sex with a Latin dance instructor who wears taps on his feet | 23 |
| Being dragged into a burning building by a cowardly dog named Herman | 12 |
| Sex with a virile renegade | 25 |

# Dreaming

| Activity | Calories burned |
|---|---|
| Regular dream | 2 |
| Wet dream | 16 |
| *(Add five calories if it occurs while in bed with your partner; add twenty calories if your partner notices.)* | |
| Dry dream | 1 |
| Wet trance | 20 |
| *(Usually occurs in the presence of a sensual hypnotist.)* | |

# Group Sex

| Activity | Calories burned |
|---|---|
| Introducing yourself | 3 |
| Overcoming shyness | 8 |
| Swapping partners | |
|   Willingly | 4 |
|   Unwillingly | 62 |
| Jealousy (partner having more fun than you are) | 16 |
| Mixed doubles | 26 |
| Being nice to everyone | 100 |
| Identity crisis | 18 |
| Anger | 10 |

(You suddenly realize that you're wanted for your body and not your mind. Difficult to cope with, especially if you have a PhD.)

| | |
|---|---|
| Finding your clothes | 5 |

# Masturbation

| Activity | Calories burned |
|---|---|
| For pleasure only | 6 |
| For exercise, too | 10 |
| For relief from tension | 12 |
| To pass the time | 7 |
| To avoid overeating | 16 |
| To get in touch with inner self | 10 |
| To get in touch with outer self | $10\frac{1}{4}$ |
| To avoid insanity | 24 |
| To avoid spending money on a date | 9 |

In addition to being a viable alternative to television, shopping and binges, masturbation is a quick and inexpensive way to get warm.

Using
Your hand(s): regular way............................11
     behind the back .....................500
     your finger(s) .........................9
Tweezers ................................................2
An inflatable doll named Heidi .....................24
A hand mike ........................................14
Tight dungarees ....................................17
Any fruit or vegetable (except watermelon
 or a sprig of parsley) ...........................19
A sandwich (no mayo, hold the lettuce) .............15
A shower massage....................................5
A vibrator:
    hand-operated .........................12
    windup.................................9
    electric ...............................5
    diesel (still in testing stages)...............74

Anything not mentioned above.......................50

In a pornographic cinema:
 Purchasing ticket ...............................$2\frac{1}{2}$
 Finding isolated seat before eyes adjust to darkness ...78
 Tripping and stumbling ...........................50
 Adjusting raincoat ...............................3

# Fetishism

There is nothing abnormal about complementing one's sexual activities with objects generally found in a less erotic setting. Certain people, for example, achieve total gratification only when wearing linoleum shoes. Others prefer foreplay with sailors who wax their legs. An erotic devotion to items such as leather, copper, dough and stockings merely suggests that you think for yourself instead of following others. For additional weight loss, try one of the popular fetishes below:

| Activity | Calories burned |
|---|---|
| Sex with a partner wearing armour | 472 |
| Sex while wearing a rubber watch | 9 |
| Sex on a three-inch merry-go-round | 146 |
| Any kipper fetish | 23 |
| Sex in a frog outfit | 58 |
| Sex with a partner wearing leather body boots | 97 |

# Bondage

Along with enhancing the sexual experience, bondage will also prevent a gluttonous partner from eating all the food. A reliable bondage device can be anything from a nylon stocking or a length of industrial chain to an ultrasophisticated restraint system such as a roll of adhesive tape and suspenders.

| *Activity* | *Calories burned* |
| --- | --- |
| Binding partner with rope (the following knots are favourites): | |
| Sheepshank | 7 |
| Slipknot | 8 |
| Half hitch | 9 |
| Figure eight | 11 |
| Square knot | 12 |
| Binding partner with a necktie | |
| Windsor knot | 9 |
| Half Windsor | 4½ |
| For the awkward, we suggest | |
| Handcuffs | 3 |
| Shackles | 6 |
| Leg irons | 5 |
| Glue | 10 |
| Escapage | |
| Struggling to get free while partner is tickling your feet | 41 |
| Untying knots | |
| Using fingernails | 7 |
| Without using fingernails | 22 |

# Discipline

An excellent high-calorie activity, especially if your partner objects.

| Activity | Calories burned |
| --- | --- |
| Thrashing partner with | |
| Ice lolly stick | 2 |
| Shoelace | 2 |
| *(add another ten calories if still in shoe)* | |
| Chopstick | 4 |
| Tongue depressor | 4 |
| Chicken wing | 6 |
| *(add twelve calories if still attached to chicken)* | |
| Oar | 15 |
| Drive shaft of a luxury car | 20 |

# Whipping

*(Making Whippie)*

| Activity | Calories burned |
|---|---|
| Using high-quality whip (per stroke) .................. 3 | |

Includes handle made of Italian leather wrapped around ebony, good balance and a built-in AM/FM radio. Gucci makes a very stylish initialled lash.

| | |
|---|---|
| Using cat-o'-nine-tails ............................... 27 | |
| Flogging a moving hen ............................... 10 | |

# Weight Loss Bonus No. 5

| Activity | Calories burned |
|---|---|

Spanking (per spank) .................................5

The most simple and satisfying form of spanking is laying your partner across your knees and then smacking the buttocks with an open hand. (In order to avert tragedy, make sure that your partner is lying face down.) Should your hand grow tired, feel free to use your partner's. For a significant increase in calories burned, slightly alter the above procedure by holding partner across your knees while you remain standing.

For those too exhausted for whipping, spanking, beating and similar manual tasks, but who still wish to enjoy some sort of discipline, we suggest relaxing in bed and just ordering your partner around. This requires little effort and saves much wear and tear on skin and bones.

Giving partner any of the following orders ..............3
  'Attention!'
  'Bring me a biscuit, slave!'
  'Bite the carpet!'
  'Polish my feet!'
  'Hop around the room, on your hands!'
As a substitute for any of the above, you can scold your partner for imagined infractions.

**Note:** If partner is also tired, he or she can pretend to obey your orders by answering, 'OK,' without actually moving a muscle.

# Sex with Animals

| Activity | Calories burned |
|---|---|
| A grateful sheep | 22 |
| An irate warthog | 150 |
| A love-starved donkey | 100 |
| An eagle in flight | 583 |
| A virile field mouse | ¼ |
| A shy chicken | 2 |
| Any fish less than fourteen inches long | 3 |
| A graceful moose | 79 |

Those who can't take criticism occasionally turn to the animal kingdom in their time of need, since the prospect of being scolded or having to make idle conversation is virtually nil.* The only drawbacks are a lack of meaningful communication and, in the case of larger animals such as lions, the danger of being eaten. Additionally, a noted sex therapist, in her book *Night at the Zoo*, maintains that forcing an animal to have sex against its will can have severe psychological repercussions, for the animal.

*You may occasionally have to say 'Whoa!' or 'Here, boy!'

# Bizarre Sex Practices

| Activity | Calories burned |
| --- | --- |
| Having partner jump on your face | 70 |
| Holding false teeth in hand and giving partner love bites | 18 |
| Foreplay while snorkelling | 100 |
| Sex on a vibrating bed | 46 |

Vibrating beds are usually found in motels frequented by people with back trouble. Look for a motel with a sign saying, 'Welcome People with Back Trouble'. These beds are activated either by dropping a coin in the slot or, if you're cheap, jumping the wires. Avoid vibrating beds if you've just eaten a lot of chili.

# Gay Sex

| Activity | Calories burned |
|---|---|
| Jolly foreplay | 4 |
| Light-hearted impotence | 1 |
| Jaunty erection | 3 |
| Hilarious coitus | 6 |
| Reckless positions | 6 |
| Lively moaning | 2 |
| Shouting with joy | 3 |
| Madcap orgasm | 7 |
| Jocular ejaculation | 5 |
| Post-orgasmic rejoicing | 6 |
| Genial fatigue | 2 |
| Convulsing partner with a joke | 3 |
| Rolling on floor with laughter | 4 |
| Rolling on partner with laughter | 6 |
| Good-natured sadism | 8 |
| Buoyant bondage | 7 |
| Dancing on the bed | 10 |

# Additional Erotic Experiences

(*For 'quickie' weight loss*)

| Activity | Calories burned |
| --- | --- |
| Watch partner shave | 4 |
| Drink from a whirlpool | 10 |
| Eat a 1-pound square of fudge, with tweezers | 40 |
| Study an Irish cookbook | 1 |
| Smoke an unfiltered herring | 13 |
| Roll around nude in a bakery window | 72 |
| Wink each other off | 90 |
| Close a business deal | 50 |
| Caress your stereo system | 30 |
| Lick a Porsche all over | 100 |
| Cook a fifteen-course dinner together without using any utensils | 80 |
| Have sex on vinyl sheets | 18 |
| Hold a Tupperware party | 82 |
| Tape-record your love cries and play them for your dentist | 51 |

# Keeping a Journal

In addition to this book, maintaining your own record of sexual activity will be helpful for keeping track of weight loss. You needn't go into great detail; just list the activity and the number of calories burned. A typical entry in a woman's journal—for example—for a pleasant, low-key sexual experience might read as follows:

## June 1: Sex with Harold

| *Activity* | *Calories burned* |
| --- | --- |
| Explaining how | 12 |
| Suggesting something different | 3 |
| Calming terrified Harold | 40 |
| Encouraging him to at least take off his socks | 8 |
| Foreplay (a little of this, a little of that) | 56 |
| Intercourse | |
| Standing position | 22 |
| Holding Harold up | 10 |
| Urging him on | 5 |
| Orgasm | not sure |
| Thanking Harold | 3 |
| Waving bye-bye | 1 |

Total time: six minutes (taxi waiting)

| *Total Calories Burned* | 160 |
| --- | --- |

# 7

# Miscellaneous Problems, Emergencies And Disasters

*'Most serious accidents occur within 50 miles of home.'\**
CHAUNCEY FARNUM, CLU

The following pages list the calories burned when coping with stress situations often encountered during sex, including shock, anxiety, fear, annoyance and discomfort. All are easily survivable if you have a sense of humour, or can get dressed quickly.

\*There are exceptions. A Persian tourist fell off her bike in Los Angeles and a fat American tore his pants while positioning himself on a barstool in Ezio's Clam Bar, Rome, Italy.

# Penis Envy

| Activity | Calories burned |
| --- | --- |
| For woman | 3 |
| For man | 72 |

# Typical Sex-Related Fears

*(Rational and irrational)*

| Activity | Calories burned |
| --- | --- |
| Partner hates me for what I did | 4 |
| Partner hates me for what I didn't do | 8 |
| At any moment my grandparents will enter the room and quietly sit down | 5 |
| Forgetting the instructions in the sex manual | 10 |
| Climaxing too soon | 5 |
| Climaxing too late | 6 |
| Not climaxing | 20 |
| Partner thinks of me as a sex object | 9 |
| Partner doesn't think of me as a sex object | 47 |
| Partner will neglect to administer last rites should I not recover from orgasm | 88 |

# Personal Fears

Some shortcomings, real and imagined, that your partner might be noticing:

| Activity | Calories burned |
|---|---|
| Breath smells like a wino's hat | 4 |
| Gigantic cellulites that shake and ripple during orgasm | 6 |
| Stretchmarks that look like a ploughed field | 8 |
| Large pores | 5 |
| No pores | 10 |
| Poorly capped teeth that wiggle | 11 |
| Excessive hair under arms | 3 |
| A roll of fat around the middle that becomes especially prominent when you sit down | 20 |
| Body odour of a disgruntled yak | 25 |

**Note:** It has been pointed out that people who were toilet trained late (teens to early twenties) have a remarkable fear of everything.

# Guilt

*(Frequently used by masochists to compensate for happiness.)*

| Activity | Calories burned |
| --- | --- |
| From | |
| Masturbation | 10 |
| Liking sex | 7 |
| Loving sex | 20 |
| Never wanting to stop except to take your temperature | 30 |
| Possible guilt situations | |
| Despite almost no formal training, orgasm comes easily, naturally and spontaneously | 53 |
| You're enjoying sex, despite the fact that other people are starving | 2 |
| Sex on your lunch hour | 3 |
| And you put it on your expense report | 20 |

# Aggravation

Although science has yet to determine precisely why aggravation burns calories, we do know that people, when aggravated, lose weight—possibly because they stamp their feet. Below are several typical situations encountered during sex.

| Activity | Calories burned |
| --- | --- |
| Partner keeps showing you his/her plants | 5 |
| Partner insists on cuddling dog during foreplay | 14 |
| Partner just visited bathroom for seventh time | 10 |
| Partner is taking phone calls | 7 |
| Partner is making phone calls | 40 |
| Partner refuses to remove jewellery, including watch, stickpin, I D bracelet, locket and flea collar | 20 |

# More Aggravation

| Activity | Calories burned |
| --- | --- |
| Rejection ............................................. 24 | |

*It is a sign of rejection if partner:*

- Insists that you keep your feet out the window
- Brings a bottle of champagne with a screw-off cap
- Attempts shock therapy with a toaster
- Attempts to rob you
- Tries to make the bed during foreplay
- Serves warm lemonade
- Asks you to take down the rubbish bin
- Sharpens a knife on the side of your head
- Doesn't remove gloves
- Tries to fold your fingers the wrong way
- Keeps sending telegrams
- Puts a bear trap on the pillow

# Acquiring Bedsores

| Activity | Calories burned |
| --- | --- |
| In bed | 20 |
| On a cheap carpet | 5 |
| On any surface generally used for industrial purposes | $\frac{1}{2}$ |

The danger of contracting bedsores from prolonged sexual activity is not remote, especially since bedsores are highly contagious. Indeed, couples have been known to emerge from bed, each of them covered by a large and hideous wound that extended from the nape of the neck to the Achilles tendon. To avoid this, partners are urged to de-bed at least once every hour, place sheets in the freezer, and perform at least ten minutes of exercises such as stretching, push-ups, sit-ups and backflips.

**Note:** Bedsores can also be avoided by generous application of car wax, olive oil or Pledge. In the case of especially severe bedsores, a slice of pizza has been known to make an effective poultice.

# Getting Caught

| Activity | Calories burned |
| --- | --- |
| By partner's spouse | 60 |
| By your spouse | $60\frac{1}{2}$ |
| Trying to explain | 165 |
| Stuttering | 28 |
| Throwing up | 40 |

Calorie counts here are flexible, depending on type of spouse—whether understanding and open-minded, or narrow-minded and armed.

# Almost Getting Caught

| Activity | Calories burned |
| --- | --- |
| Trying to remain calm | 100 |
| Fright (includes trembling) | 66 |
| Leaping out of bed | 25 |
| Getting dressed in one large motion | 300 |
| Thanking partner quickly | 2 |
| Jumping out of window | 15 |
| (*Add five calories if window wasn't open.*) | |
| Landing | 1 |
| Running very fast | 50 |

# Threatening Situations

| Activity | Calories burned |
|---|---|
| Partner arrives wearing a leather leisure suit and sipping from a can of motor oil | 34 |
| Partner has brought a relative | 40 |
| Partner's slave fetish is getting out of hand | 50 |
| A surreptitious three-hour search fails to turn up partner's alleged vasectomy scar | 100 |

# Interruptions and Distractions

| Activity | Calories burned |
| --- | --- |
| Somebody going peek-a-boo | 15 |
| Noisy neighbours | 7 |
| Skipping record | 5 |
| Excessive moonlight | 1 |
| Skipping child | 10 |
| Partner wearing a silly hat | 6 |
| Telephone | 4 |
| Flock of geese | 11 |
| War | 70 |
| Bed catches fire | 15 |
| Hunger | 9 |
| Ice-cream man ringing bells | 14 |
| Knock on door (Jehovah's Witness selling *The Watchtower*). | 10 |
| Resuming where you left off | 30 |

# Afflictions

A common affliction that strikes without warning.
It generally afflicts those who attempt a position that
conflicts with the laws of gravity or who have not
warmed up sufficiently (see Chapter 1). The result is
a pressing need to straighten out the leg
immediately, even if it means kicking your partner,
falling on the floor and turning orgasm into a
terrifying experience.

**Note:** Hay fever sufferers would do well to avoid having sex
in a field of ragweed or in dusty bookshops.

# Call of Nature

| Activity | Calories burned |
|---|---|
| Going and getting it over with | 8 |
| Gritting teeth and holding out until you can't stand the pain | 100 |

Nothing is more miserable than leaving a nice warm bed containing another nice warm body just to perform a chore. On the other hand, remaining in bed and hoping it will somehow go away never works, no matter how hard you pray.

**Note:** If your partner agrees, you can keep a porcelain potty under the bed for emergencies.

# Fighting off Pets

| Activity | Calories burned |
| --- | --- |
| Tiny nervous dogs weighing less than eight ounces | 3 |
| Playful Saint Bernard | 20 |
| Jealous Doberman | 92 |
| Any enraged mongrel | 50 |
| Cat | 6 |
| Resentful parakeet | $2\frac{1}{2}$ |

Although a determined sweep of the hand will usually work, we advocate a pistol, club or terrifically loud voice.

# Assorted Accidents

| Activity | Calories burned |
| --- | --- |
| **Toupee slips off** | |
| If partner knew you were wearing one | 6 |
| If partner didn't know | 72 |
| **Passionate moaning causes dentures to fall out** | 28 |
| **Extinguishing cigarette** | |
| In ashtray | 1 |
| In mattress | 17 |
| In partner's leg | 133 |
| **Calling partner by wrong name** | 50 |
| **Bed collapses** | 10 |
| **Shorts explode during foreplay** | 90 |

# 8

---

# Eating and Sex
## (The Bedside Eater)

*'Sex to nourish the soul, food to nourish the sex.'*
  KARL 'CARL' SCHUSSELDORF,
  NUTRITIONIST

Advanced thinkers have long been aware that the nutritional requirements of sex are, to say the least, awesome. Not only does intense sexual activity deprive the body of height and weight, but also causes a rapid depletion of proteins, carbohydrates, riboflavin, oxygen, cereal fillers and vital minerals such as copper, zinc and aluminium. If these essential elements are not replaced soon, rigor mortis sets in and we begin to grow irritable. We must therefore recognize the importance of taking nourishment during any period of sexual activity exceeding fifteen minutes, lest we do irreversible damage to organs, glands and bone marrow.

We must not, however, undo the good work done thus far by stuffing ourselves with high caloric and fattening foods such as halvah, creamed spinach, biscuits and bean soup. Nor should we go to the other extreme; rigid dieting invites misery, and puritans who consider a cup of tea and polyunsaturated bean sprouts nutritionally sound generally suffer a premature death. There is no harm in relaxing our dietary vigil providing we do so with intelligence, seeking a happy medium between utter starvation and sheer piggery.

Best for bedside eating are foods that enhance the sexual experience—high energy aphrodisiacs containing the minimum adult daily requirement of satisfaction and yielding a high rate of pleasure per calorie: chocolate cake, ice cream (most flavours), caviar, chili con carne, pizza, spareribs and authentic ethnic foods such as Chinese, Italian, French and American. This, as opposed to foods yielding a vile rate of satisfaction per calorie: okra, biscuits, parsley, watercress, Spam and codfish cakes. Mention should also be made of the fraudulent aphrodisiacs: Spanish fly, oysters, baby food, wheat germ, chicken pot pie, prunes and porridge, all of which are useless. And, finally, we counsel against what are capriciously known as 'health' foods, most of which contribute to acute famishment, pellagra and depression.

The following refreshments were chosen by a panel of experts as those most often partaken of before, during, after—and way after—sex. These foods and beverages are held in high esteem not only for their nutritional value, but for their good taste and salubrious effect upon the psyche. If you happen to keep a small refrigerator beside the bed, so much the better. It will make the job of taking nourishment that much more convenient. As always, we recommend prudent indulgence, and never have sex directly after a heavy meal.*

---

*A heavy meal: truffled sausages, pâté, clam chowder (two bowls), meat loaf and chips with green ravioli al Forno, assorted goat cheeses, four pieces of fudge, beer, wine and Perrier. Dessert: a one-inch pizza (unsweetened) with everything on it.

# Calories in Food

*(Calorie counts listed below will vary according to ingredients, size of portion and dimensions of mouth.)*

| Food | Calories |
| --- | --- |

Ice cream
    Per spoonful ........................................14
    Per ladleful .........................................84

'Plasma for the soul,' is how one eating specialist expressed her reverence for ice cream as she slowly demolished her second pint of rum raisin. Since the Renaissance, ice cream has been worshipped for its healing powers and ability to effect miraculous recoveries in people suffering from backache, tonsillitis, impotence, enlarged sweet tooth and other major disorders. In order to savour its fullest essence, ice cream should be eaten or sipped directly from the container, instead of placing it in a dish and risking contamination. This is especially important with flavours such as butter almond and pistachio, where too much handling may bruise the nuts. Many ice cream fetishists, in order to prevent melting and 'flavour leakage' between store and home, transport their purchase in a refrigerated hat.

Creamsicle (per lick) ...................................3
A highly portable, easy-to-eat item that is suitable should you want some ice cream during intercourse. Be careful that it doesn't melt and drip into your partner's eye. After finishing use the stick for discipline (see Chapter VI).

Frozen custard

Per lick .........................................$3\frac{1}{4}$

Will do in a crisis, although it will probably melt all
over your wrist. If you have the time, and need the
exercise, go over to the dispenser, affix your
mouth directly to the nozzle and ingest a pint or two
without bothering with a cone.

Pizza (per bite) ...................................15

Builds strong bones and teeth. If you order your
pizza with extra cheese, meatballs, anchovies,
mushrooms and pepperoni (known as the 'Breath-
burner Surprise'), add a few calories. Although pizza
is just a bit clumsy to eat in bed, especially if it's hot
and you insert the entire slice into your mouth at once,
it is an excellent source of potassium and vitamin D.
Always order pizza well in advance and have your
money ready. Fumbling for correct change while the
delivery person waits in the hall and your partner
waits in bed can make you feel foolish.*

Leftover spaghetti (per strand) ........................3

This, too, is somewhat difficult to eat in bed, but the
nutritional benefits are well worth it. Like good wine,
a well-aged spaghetti (sixteen to eighteen hours) can
make a glorious addition to bedroom cuisine, a
delicate yet substantial repast that helps the body
maintain its vim and vigour, no matter what. If you've
added meatballs, so much the better. You can throw
them at each other should you grow bored.

*In certain counties, a pizza delivery is considered to be a valid
medical emergency and delivery trucks are equipped with sirens.

Cold meat loaf (per handful) ........................14
A stick-to-the-bedsheets dish that provides the
necessary stamina for long-distance sex. Meat loaf is
generally served with chips, but in this case, we prefer
something a bit lighter, like soy beans. Weight-
watchers take note: Cold meat loaf contains 1 per cent
fewer calories than warm meat loaf.

Brownie or fudge (per hearty nibble) ..................28
Like ice cream, the restorative powers of brownies
and fudge make them an indispensable part of bedroom
eating. Indeed, one huge brownie, with a coating of
perfect fudge (an 'oxygen' brownie) pulled one
couple out of a trance brought on by two days of steady
sex, during which time they stopped only once to
change the bed.

Cherries (per cherry, no stem) ........................2½
One of the most refreshing of fruits, especially when
served cold. Keep a spare cherry in your navel for
emergencies and decoration. It will please your
partner. Note: Cherries, which are rich in vitamin C,
will help prevent scurvy.

Caviar:
Per ounce ......................................91
Per egg ...................................00.00047

Erotically exotic and exotically erotic. Don't waste
caviar on a second-rate partner. Wait until after
you've had sex. If your partner wasn't any good, serve
crisps instead. Caviar should be washed down with
either champagne or a suitable substitute such as
Dr Brown's Cel-Ray tonic.

Mars bar (per bite) ................................20
Because of its sublime chewability, Mars is
considered to be a supreme example of dental
satisfaction and the perfect flesh substitute,
should you become tired of biting into your partner.
It is one of the few chocolate bars that will accept a
love bite.

Pâté (per smear) ................................22
One of the most life-giving and sensuous of spreads is
a country pâté comprised of veal, pork, brandy and
garlic. It can be eaten directly from the knife, or, if
you don't mind a few extra calories, smeared on bread.
To revive those in the final stages of starvation, a
renowned eating tutor suggests digging a trench in a
two-foot loaf of French bread, packing it with pâté
and, as he so eloquently puts it, 'Stuffing your face
until you faint.'

Bread (per one-pound loaf) ....................1115.3
If you are finicky, you may wish to cut the loaf into
what dainty eaters call 'slices,' and then figure your
calories accordingly. Healthy eaters, however, know
the value of a good dose of bread and generally prefer
to cut the loaf in half, hollow out the inside and fill it
with peanut butter, eggplant or tuna fish.

Cheese (per hunk) ................................30
For quick energy and performing nibbling
exercises, a plate of assorted cheeses, all served at
room temperature, should be a fundamental part of
the bedroom repast. Sharp Cheddar, Brie, Edam,
Gruyère and Roquefort are most recommended.

Miniature chocolate eggs (per egg) ....................21
    No matter how tired or hungry you are, do not
    neglect to remove the foil or you'll be sorry,
    especially if you are in the midst of root canal work.
    Besides tasting good, chocolate eggs are excellent for
    raising the blood sugar to an acceptable level.
    Hypoglycemiacs take note.

Chocolate cake (per bite) ...........................26
    One of the few reliable cures for sexual
    dysfunction. In fact, the therapeutic effect of
    chocolate cake is such that people have been known
    to eat large slices of it even when they're not
    having sex.

Chili con carne (per spoonful) ......................10
    Vital for energy and unusual dreams. A crock of
    chili should be kept alongside the bed, to be dipped
    into whenever you get sleepy. Don't worry about the
    after-effects. The additional carbon dioxide will be
    good for your plants.

Cheesecake (per forkful) ...........................24
    Many consider cheesecake to be an orgasm unto
    itself and frequently use it as a partner substitute.
    Although there is significant controversy over the
    merits of Italian versus French cheesecake, we
    suggest both.

Westphalian smoked ham (per thin slice)....,..........11
    The erotic counterpart of baloney. It is generally
    served wrapped around either a slice of chilled
    honeydew or your finger.

Cold seafood salad (per large spoonful) ..............18
    The perfect fuel for warm-weather sex. It is light,
    nourishing and, if you eat enough, acceptably filling.

Potato pancakes (per bite) ........................25
One of the less epicurean of the bedroom foods, but essential for roughage and building strength—it is a favourite dish of Jewish field hands. Those who have difficulty keeping warm will find potato pancakes a blessing. Once swallowed, they burn like peat, enabling one to easily maintain normal body temperature during sex in a walk-in freezer.

Chocolate biscuits (per bite) ........................8
By no means intended as a total dietary programme. However, thirty-five chocolate biscuits stored under the pillow and 'popped' at appropriate times will serve to maintain a proper balance between the red and white blood cells. Most healthful type of biscuits are those made by a caring mother, or, if one is not available, a doting aunt. During emergencies, store-purchased biscuits will do.

Wine (per sip) ..................................... 10
> The rule here is simplicity itself. White with a thin
> partner, red with a heavy partner, rosé with a bore. As
> for serving wine with food, make up your own rules,
> depending on your own taste and the ignorance of
> your partner. You'll find that most wines with a
> grape base go with almost any kind of food. A
> chilled Chablis, for example, will work just as well
> with meat loaf as it will with gefilte fish. We do
> advise, however, against muscatel with oysters
> Rockefeller and Manischewitz with pork cutlets.

Beer:
> (per sip) ....................................... 8
> (per gulp) ..................................... 14

> Ice cold beer is a dependable antidote to long,
> gruelling hours of hot, sweaty sex. An ideal way to
> replace vital body fluids, beer is also rich in
> vitamins, minerals and carbon dioxide. For extra
> nutritive power, try dark beer, copious doses of
> which will give you the strength to sit up and eat.
> Beer stands up especially well to such formidable
> dishes as saddle of lamb, chili con carne, hot dogs *en
> gelée*, goulash and any type of sausage.

Champagne (per tight little sip) ...................... 8
> Depending upon taste, pocketbook and how you feel
> about your partner, you can opt for anything from
> a $1.99 bottle of Cold Duck to a $15.99 bottle of
> Taittinger. Champagne for bedroom consumption
> should not be restricted to 'luxury' foods such as
> caviar and chili. Piper Heidseck served with meat
> loaf has been known to alleviate frigidity and
> Mumm's with yams is a popular calmative for those
> upset by inadequate foreplay.

Perrier mineral water ................................0
    Known in some circles as the perfect water
    substitute, this gently gaseous, highly cultured
    liquid can be taken straight or with a twist of
    lemon.

Sodas (sweetened, per swallow).....................14
    If carbonated beverage abuse is your thing, we
    suggest the Bordeaux of sodas, Royal Crown Cola
    for its rich, eye-watering flavour and polished
    elegance. If Royal Crown isn't available in your area,
    try Pepsi-Cola, a bit thinner but a dependable
    choice. Soda should be uncapped and allowed to
    stand for at least two minutes before serving.

# Typical Effects of Alcohol on Bedroom Behaviour*

*One ounce of alcohol.* Little effect. Head still clear, breath not bad. Pulse, breathing and liver normal. Can still satisfy partner.

*Two to three ounces.* Still pretty much know what you're there for but it somehow doesn't matter. You're growing relaxed, almost tranquil. You don't complain when partner tries to sell you a raffle ticket. Sense of humour still crisp. Fashioning a monocle by holding a biscuit to your eye strikes you as unbearably funny.

*Four ounces.* Minor problem differentiating between bed and floor. Hope partner doesn't notice. Growing feeling of queasiness vanishes when you take a meatball. Changing position brings it back, however, and you suddenly become sick. Partner is gracious and pretends not to notice. Curious urge to boil the bed.

*Five to six ounces.* Still in control, but ability to perform simple sexual tasks such as drooling and moaning impeded by blinding headache. One of you had an orgasm a few moments ago but you can't remember who. Vision and tactile sensitivity slightly distorted. Cannot locate partner except by listening for a voice. By now you are belching uncontrollably and the dog is cowering in the corner.

*Eight to nine ounces.* Tongue feels like luncheon meat. Though functionally dead, you find the concept of playing a wind instrument by holding it up to a fan profoundly fascinating. Unaware that partner has departed, you begin a heated argument with the pillow over who should go for ice cream.

*From *New Perspectives on the Relationship Between Alcohol and Silly Behaviour*, by Dr Erica Einstein, Professor of Home Economics, University of the Transvaal.

# Examples of Weight Lost While Eating

| Activity | Calories burned |
| --- | ---: |
| Hunger pangs | $\frac{1}{2}$ |
| Opening refrigerator door | 1 |
| Shuffling through nonessentials (celery, jelly, egg, lemons, torch batteries, etc.) | 2 |

Raising fork containing:
| | |
| --- | ---: |
| Good, solid meatball | 4 |
| Stringy piece of boiled chicken | 2 |
| Italian cheesecake | 16 |
| Consommé | 00.000006 |

| | |
| --- | ---: |
| Prying lid from inadequately thawed pint of ice cream (includes mangled fingernails) | 21 |

Sliding spoon into:
| | |
| --- | ---: |
| Ice cream thawed to creamy consistency | 2 |

*(only the gentlest of pressure should be needed, let gravity do the rest)*

| | |
| --- | ---: |
| Ice cream just taken from freezer | 76 |

*(includes turning red and panting)*

| | |
| --- | ---: |
| Unbending spoon | 6 |

**Note:** If you cannot wait for ice cream to melt, use the 'shovel' method and stand on the spoon. This will drive the spoon in far enough to give you enough leverage to dislodge an 'emergency' portion.

| | |
| --- | ---: |
| Spreading peanut butter on bread | 3 |
| Dipping bread into jar and scooping out peanut butter | 1 |
| Separating the halves of lemon creme biscuit without breaking them | 4 |

Licking off the creme ...................................2

Removing cork from wine bottle:
  With corkscrew ....................................7
  Violent sucking ..................................145
  Hitting bottom of bottle with heel of hand ..........65

Chewing (per chew):
  Foods such as applesauce, salads, soups ..............1
  Cheap cuts of meat ...............................11
  Caramel ..........................................14

Eating pizza:
  Slice folded .......................................4
  Not folded .......................................25
Sucking on pizza tin until it buckles (extreme hunger) ....98

Removing wrapper from any chocolate bar:
  Gently, with fingers ................................1
  Tearing it off with teeth ...........................$\frac{1}{2}$
  Burning it off ....................................$\frac{1}{4}$

Trimming the fat from fish............................2

Running to catch slowly-pulling-away ice-cream
van ................................................40

Eating spaghetti using:
  Spoon and fork ...................................6
  Cupped hands ....................................15

# Weight Lost While Resisting Food

People who insist on rigid dieting, even during sex, will be happy to learn that exercising willpower burns considerable calories. The more tempting the food, of course, the more energy needed to successfully resist.

| Activity | Calories burned |
|---|---|
| Resisting: | |
| Apple pie with vanilla ice cream | 65 |
| A soft-boiled egg | $\frac{1}{4}$ |
| Lettuce | 1 |
| Shrimp in lobster sauce | 28 |
| Mars bar | 30 |
| Spaghetti and meatballs | |
|    Homemade | 55 |
|    From a can | 2 |
| Beans | $\frac{1}{2}$ |
| Cheesecake | 58 |
| Chocolate cake | 72 |
| Shredded wheat | 00.00004 |
| Frozen chicken pie | 4 |
| Ice cream | 187 |
| Toblerone | 19 |
| Cherry pie | 40 |
| Broth | 0 |

# Eating in Bed—Problems

| Activity | Calories burned |
| --- | --- |
| Sticking together | 5 |
| Prying yourselves apart | 14 |

Removing food stains from sheet:
  Ice cream:

| | |
| --- | --- |
| Chocolate | 5 |
| Vanilla | don't worry about it |
| Red wine | 8 |
| Tomato sauce | 6 |
| Oil from pizza | 11 |
| Ground-in meat | 8 |

**Note:** Food stains should be regarded as symbols of fun, much like the decals people paste on their car windows to show they've been to Longleat.

| | |
| --- | --- |
| Bedsores | 5 |

Moving back and forth on a sheet filled with bread crumbs, peanut shells, cherry stones and potato crisps will cause tender skin to become irritated. Always hoover between courses.

| | |
| --- | --- |
| Sharing a bowl of soup during intercourse | 80 |

# Alternate Uses of Food

Despite the danger of an allergic reaction, covering each other with food such as peanut butter, whipped cream or hot fudge, then licking it off is an excellent way to save time by combining sex with lunch. For best results, wait until you are both undressed before beginning.

| *Activity* | *Calories burned* |
| --- | --- |
| Licking off: | |
| Honey | 4 |
| Strawberry jam | 6 |
| Turkey leg | 19 |
| Chewing gum | 86 |
| Whipped cream | 2 |
| Shaving cream (good joke) | 46 |
| Grapes | 1 |
| Organic makeup | 10 |

# The Height Report

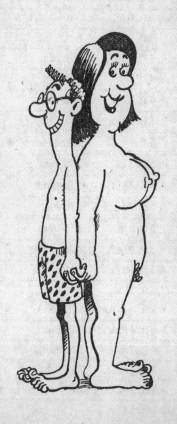

# How Tall Should the Ideal Sex Partner Be?*

(*Women over the age of twelve should add one inch to all measurements*)

If you are:  You should be:

| | Small frame | Medium frame | Large frame |
|---|---|---|---|
| 14 to 30 lbs. | 2 ft. 1 in. | 2 ft. 3 in. | 2 ft. 5 in. |
| 31 to 42 lbs. | 2 ft. 4 in. | 2 ft. 7 in. | 3 ft. |
| 43 to 54 lbs. | 2 ft. 9 in. | 3 ft. | 3 ft. 3 in. |
| 55 to 65 lbs. | 3 ft. 2 in. | 3 ft. 7 in. | 4 ft. $\frac{1}{2}$ in. |
| 66 to 77 lbs. | 3 ft. 9 in. | 4 ft. 1 in. | 4 ft. 4 in. |
| 78 to 90 lbs. | 4 ft. | 4 ft. 4 in. | 4 ft. 7 in. |
| 91 to 100 lbs. | 4 ft. 5 in. | 4 ft. 9 in. | 5 ft. |
| 101 to 110 lbs. | 4 ft. 10 in. | 5 ft. 1 in. | 5 ft. 3 in. |
| 111 to 122 lbs. | 5 ft. | 5 ft. 2 in. | 5 ft. 5 in. |
| 123 to 135 lbs. | 5 ft. 3 in. | 5 ft. 5 in. | 5 ft. 7 in. |
| 136 to 147 lbs. | 5 ft. 3$\frac{1}{2}$ in. | 5 ft. 6 in. | 5 ft. 9 in. |
| 148 to 160 lbs. | 5 ft. 7 in. | 5 ft. 9 in. | 5 ft. 11 in. |
| 161 to 172 lbs. | 5 ft. 8 in. | 5 ft. 10 in. | 6 ft. $\frac{1}{4}$ in. |
| 173 to 185 lbs. | 5 ft. 9 in. | 6 ft. | 6 ft. 2 in. |
| 186 to 200 lbs. | 5 ft. 10 in. | 6 ft. 1 in. | 6 ft. 4 in. |
| 201 to 212 lbs. | 5 ft. 11 in. | 6 ft. 2 in. | 6 ft. 5 in. |
| 213 to 225 lbs. | 6 ft. | 6 ft. 3 in. | 6 ft. 7 in. |
| 226 to 240 lbs. | 6 ft. 4 in. | 6 ft. 6 in. | 6 ft. 10 in. |
| 241 to 255 lbs. | 6 ft. 7 in. | 6 ft. 10 in. | 7 ft. 2 in. |
| 256 to 270 lbs. | 7 ft. $\frac{1}{2}$ in. | 7 ft. 3 in. | 7 ft. 7 in. |
| 271 to 285 lbs. | 7 ft. 3 in. | 7 ft. 7 in. | 8 ft. |

*Based on certain tables.